The Platonic Myths

Other works by Josef Pieper from St. Augustine's Press

The Christian Idea of Man

The Concept of Sin

Death and Immortality

Enthusiasm and Divine Madness: On the Platonic Dialogue Phaedrus

Happiness and Contemplation

In Tune with the World: A Theory of Festivity

Scholasticism: Personalities and Problems of Medieval Philosophy

The Silence of Goethe

The Silence of St. Thomas: Three Essays

Tradition: Concept and Claim

What Catholics Believe (with Heinz Kastop)

Other titles of interest

C.S. Lewis and Don Giovanni Calabria, *The Latin Letters of C.S. Lewis*

Servais Pinckaers, O.P., *Morality: The Catholic View*

Peter Kreeft, *The Philosophy of Jesus*

Peter Kreeft, *Jesus-Shock*

Peter Kreeft, *The Sea Within: Waves and the Meaning of All Things*

Peter Kreeft, *I Surf, Therefore I Am: A Philosophy of Surfing*

Robert Hugh Benson, *Lord of the World*

James V. Schall, *The Modern Age*

James V. Schall, *The Regensburg Lecture*

James V. Schall, *The Sum Total of Human Happiness*

Nalin Ranasinghe, *Socrates in the Underworld: On Plato's* Gorgias

The Platonic Myths

Josef Pieper

Introduction by James V. Schall
Translated by Dan Farrelly

ST. AUGUSTINE'S PRESS
South Bend, Indiana
2011

Manufactured in the United States of America

1 2 3 4 5 6   16 15 14 13 12 11

Library of Congress Cataloging in Publication Data
Pieper, Josef, 1904–1997.
[Über die Platonischen Mythen. English]
The Platonic myths / Josef Pieper; introduction by
James V. Schall; translated by Dan Farrelly. – 1st ed.
p. cm.
Originally published: Über die Platonischen Mythen.
Munich : Kösel-Verlag KG, 1965.
Includes bibliographical references and index.
ISBN 978-1-58731-636-4 (clothbound: alk. paper) –
ISBN 978-1-58731-637-1 (pbk: alk. paper)
1. Plato. 2. Mythology, Greek. I. Title.
B398.M8P5 2010
184 – dc22   2010029894

∞ *The paper used in this publication meets the minimum
requirements of the American National Standard for
Information Sciences – Permanence of Paper for Printed
Materials, ANSI Z39.48-1984.*

ST. AUGUSTINE'S PRESS
www.staugustine.net

TABLE OF CONTENTS

} v {

Table of Contents

VI

INTRODUCTION

Myths That Are True and
Truths Expressed in Myths

I.

AFTER DISTINGUISHING THIS THING FROM THAT, SEEKING clarity on what belongs where, Josef Pieper always puts things back together, especially the most important things. This little book, *The Platonic Myths*, is something that I have been looking for all my life, but I did not know that this was what I was looking for. I recognized it when I read it. Almost every book of Josef Pieper is, in some sense, a commentary on Plato. One of the most remarkable books I know is Pieper's *Enthusiasm and Divine Madness*, which is a commentary on the *Phaedrus*. His book *On Love* is, among other things, a commentary on Plato's *Symposium*. What Pieper says of Aristophanes' explication of love and its mythological background is crucial to the thesis of this present book.

After having read the *Republic* many, many

times, I finally saw one day, much to my surprise, what it said in Book Ten. To the annoyance of liberal thinkers of all eras, there Socrates abolished the poets from his city in speech. He seemed so heartless. What was the poets' "crime"? They (the poets) depicted much too attractively, as Adeimantus already had said in Book Two, all the divine and heroic carousers, fibbers, cut-purses, and killers in their poetic cities after death. Their attraction and disorder of soul were too striking not to notice.

From *The Apology,* moreover, we assumed that Socrates had replaced the myths with philosophy, with the rigorous knowledge of *what is.* And in fact, so he did, at least some myths. But other myths kept coming back in crucial places, particularly those in the *Phaedo,* the *Gorgias,* and the *Republic,* the eschatological myths. Plato could not set aside the ultimate fate of actual men on the basis of their record in this world. It seemed that many crimes went unpunished; many good things went unrewarded. These facts indicated serious faults in the very structure of the world.

In the city in speech that is being built in the *Republic,* however, after we have seen why many poets who charm us, including Homer and Hesiod, were abolished, we find Socrates telling us that the poets, now purified, could be permitted back in the city we are building, the best city. Not only do we need them; we delight in them. When all is in order, we sing as we should. Plato is not at all opposed to poetry. Indeed, the *Republic* itself is, at one level, a haunting poem designed to out-charm Homer at his own game.

When we see the light, let it shine on *what is*, not just shine but glorify. It has always been clear that the *Republic* of Plato and the *City of God* of Augustine, in effect, had the same title. The only thing they seemed to differ in was in the location of this city. It turns out, as Pieper argues, that they really, on essentials, do not differ at all. They are related as the foundation of a building to its completion, not as two separate buildings.

Josef Pieper has carefully read the German commentaries on myth and its history, especially as they are used in Plato. He realized that modern scholars on Plato want to read him as if his treatment of myth was not an essential element in his philosophy. Thus, it was maintained that Plato did not find anything "true" in myths. His "real" philosophy did not include them for the same reason that modern philosophy does not include them. They have nothing to teach us unless they picture something we have discovered by modern scientific investigations. Myths had nothing to teach us except practical lessons that were the point of the yarns and doings of the gods and heroes. They were but lessons and analogies.

Pieper suggests, however, that we find two sorts of myths in Plato's works. We do find myths that simply teach a lesson by an extended example. But we also find myths, those ancient ones that are handed down from of old that purport to explain the origins of man with his relation to the gods. These myths appear in various forms, often refashioned by Plato, but each seeks to find a truth that does not seem to be expressible by philosophic arguments. Again, Pieper does not think that philosophizing and myth teachings are necessarily incompatible. Quite the opposite, he thinks that human knowledge in its unaided philosophic form could only be expressed about many basic things, such as the eternity of the gods and the creation of man, in myths. Yet, these myths themselves seem to have been passed down from of yore.

II.

We learn such stories and myths "from hearing," not from argumentation. Somehow they are

Introduction

largely the same in the memories of most peoples, almost as if there was an original revelation. In the Epistle to the Hebrews, we read that God spoke in former times. We already find this understanding in Plato. Pieper's discussion of this knowledge from hearing is brilliant.

When speaking of faith in the Christian sense, Pieper often points out that we do not have faith on faith on faith *ad infinitum*. Faith does not finally bring us back to faith but to someone who sees. Christian faith brings us back to witnesses, finally to the Apostles who see Christ who sees the Father. The Platonic notion is like this seeing and testifying. It does not yet know the Father or the Son, but it records something handed on by someone or something that originally saw and heard and passed it on.

It is often maintained that the Platonic Good and the Aristotelian First Mover are incompatible with Christian revelation. Such a conclusion, however different they are, is hasty, in Pieper's view. One can speak, as several authors such as Eric Voegelin do, of Plato having received a "revelation." This receiving is what Pieper meant by tradition and its handing down certain truths in various forms but always with the same general context. There is a creator. There is an original sin. There is a redemption. It ultimately unites the men and the gods in a common community. Again, Plato does not present the Christian specifics of this understanding, but in Pieper's view what he says is in the same order. Revelation and reason are not at odds. They almost seem to be awaiting each other.

There is, it strikes me, a direct line between Pieper's explication of the myths of Plato, the thought of Augustine, the orderly relation of Trinity, man, and cosmos in Aquinas over against the break in modern political philosophy, where the transcendent order disappears. We locate the best regime in this world, precisely contrary to Plato and revelation. What can in fact reasonably be located in this world are practical regimes that take into consideration man's reason and the Fall.

We are realistic about what we can expect of actual men in actual time. We see, however, that no actual regime can be identified with man's final end. The political world, natural though it be, is an arena for a more profound drama. This drama concerns essentially justice and its accomplishment or failure to be accomplished. This is the drama that concerned Plato all his life. It constituted the core of the death of Socrates—the best man in the best existing city. Why did he not survive there?

Indeed, one might say that the heart of civilization is the Socratic principle, already found in *The Apology* and the *Crito*, that it is never right to do wrong. That given a choice between death and doing wrong, it is best to choose death, for we know not if it is evil or not in comparison to doing wrong, which we know. Modernity reintroduces the denial of this principle, already found expressed in the First Book of the *Republic* and the *Gorgias*, that we are not restricted by this limitation arising from the distinction of right and wrong. This principle is the rule of politics that constitutes modernity from Machiavelli and Hobbes.

III.

But what Pieper does here, is to bring back the eschatological Plato into the heart of politics and thereby to indicate its limits. The direct line, then, passes from the denial of eternity to the effort to replace it by political or scientific movements in this world. What Voegelin called "the imanentization of the eschaton" is what lies behind modernity. I have tried to show this line in my book, *The Modern Age*. It is remarkable how the line of

Pieper's *Platonic Myths* leads from his eschatological myths to Benedict XVI's encyclical *Spe Salvi,* which reaffirms that the modern "solution" to the best city established by science with the rejection of God has left man without his very nature and true destiny. This fury to reconstruct man is the meaning of all the efforts to extend human life for centuries, to produce human beings apart from the family, and to assert that man lacks the capacity to know and will.

The central problem in Plato's philosophy was that of whether the world was created in injustice, a topic that haunted him. The eschatological myths, as he saw them, were teachings that it was not. Pieper explains that the truth of Plato's argument in this area always ended in a "myth" that reflected an original revelation but also answered a philosophical problem of central human importance in the best way available to him. In the Myth of Er in the *Republic,* it is quite clear that the judgment of men, with immortal souls, both for punishment and reward, is necessary for the completion of a world that God created originally as good with all beings in it. It is the free being, man, in his political arena, where we see him work out his destiny. This is why politics must recover eschatology. It has tried to replace it and has made itself a self-creator with a paltry destiny.

This little book of Josef Pieper gets us to the real heart of things. It re-establishes the centrality of human freedom and human sin. How they are dealt with, in the light of human intelligence, constitutes the key project of mankind and of each person within the arena of the world. Politics has its own limited sphere, but it is never, as such, salvific, though the citizens of any regime can be lost or saved by virtue of their own knowings and doings. Plato understood that the eschatological myths that appear in his dialogues in their own way taught the truth, taught the answer to a philosophical, not mythical, problem that concerned every person who lived a human life in this world from the beginning.

Pieper brings forth remarkably in this book that some things are answers to human concerns but they are not deduced from abstract forms or essences. We do not first encounter essences walking down the street, then proceed to individuals. We first encounter human beings in action in their city, as Aristotle taught us to notice. It is from this background that we deal with the levels of being in the cosmos.

But individual persons appear outside of syllo-gistic reasoning, which is no insult to the syllo-gism. Rational beings with body and mind cannot appear from any place but from being itself, the being that is good. This is why the initial ques-tions, "Why is there something, not nothing?" "Why is this thing not that thing?" "Why is it that I am rather than am not?" are questions that first arise in a real being already there in the world and reflecting on its condition. Aristotle said that man does not make man to be man. He is already man when he first appears. He discovers; he does not make.

The reintroduction of a transcendent eschatol-ogy relates to, but is separate from, existing poli-ties. Political eschatology is now located in this world. But every soul, as Socrates says, and reve-lation reaffirms, has a transcendent destiny. This destiny is the real purpose of this born-in-time ex-istence. Plato was right, as Pieper shows and as Benedict remarks, that the judgment of the living and the dead, as found both in the Platonic myths and in the Nicene Creed, is properly speaking the completion of both the city and the cosmos in their own orders.

In the city, we seek to reward good and pun-ish evil. But we all know, as did Plato, that the punishment of the real crimes and rewards of deeds of virtue cannot have fully happened in this world, however much its judges strove for justice. The Platonic myths, in this sense, are nothing else but proper teachings and reminders of the greatness of what it is to be human, a greatness no human being initially gave to himself. But it is that to which each actual citizen in any regime is called, but achieved only if freely accepted as a gift from what is Good.

The reading of *The Platonic Myths* of Josef Pieper is a profoundly moving experience. No philosophical book brings us closer to the proper understanding how all things fit together. It is a book that excludes nothing, including revelation, from the scope of the philosophic mind. Armed with an extraordinary openness to *what is*, we discover what we really are, in the midst of our seeking the perfect kingdom in the wrong place.

– James V. Schall, s.j.
Georgetown University
February 23, 2010

The Platonic Myths

I

ANYONE WHO HAS EVEN PAGED THROUGH THE PLATONIC
dialogues knows how full of stories they are.
Above all, every dialogue is a story in itself. In the
sphere of philosophical utterance, that is a somewhat strange phenomenon. And the questions
awaiting us here are not easy to answer.

If the *Nicomachean Ethics* of Aristotle, Plato's
student, begin with the sentence: "Every art,
every teaching, every activity, every decision has
some good as its aim, so that one can rightly say
that good is what every being strives for," the
meaning is not immediately clear to today's reader
and perhaps he will not straightforwardly accept
it; but he will be quite familiar with the thrust of
this approach, which will seem to him completely
appropriate. But the idea that a book which has a
theory of the state as its theme should begin with
the description of a visit to cultic games, with de-
scriptions of processions, exhibitions, horse-riding
by torchlight, a chance meeting with old friends
who send a slave to persuade a man not to return

home (and so on) – such an idea is not immediately clear. But, as is well known, that is exactly the content of the first section of Plato's *Republic.* And it is not as if, for instance, once the dialogue situation has been established and described, the strict argumentation would take over from the story-telling. Instead, elements are continually introduced which have no logical connection; emotion comes into it; chance details from the participants' personal lives [appear], or the sudden flash of an idea which threatens to divert the theme from its central course. Above all, new stories are continually interspersed – for example, in the dialogue about the state, the story of Gyges' ring ("None of us, if we were to possess it, would be so well forearmed as not to lay hands on others' goods"[1]); the famous cave parable, which is in no way an allegorical description of a state or condition, but – and this is what Heidegger's interpretation is rightly based on,[2] – the narration of an event, and so, again, a story; finally, at the end of the dialogue,[3] the strange report of a Pamphilian soldier who lies as a corpse on the field of battle and then on the twelfth day, when he is now on the funeral pyre, comes to life again and begins to tell what he has seen – "beyond."

Does this all mean, we must ask, anything

more than that Plato is by nature a great inventor of stories, who, as Socrates says of himself, takes pleasure in telling stories and also even inventing them? Or is he above all concerned with the didactic aspect, with conveying an abstract thought through a graphic image? Is this philosophy at all and not something like literature, so that whoever wants to grasp Plato's philosophy – insofar as there is one – would have to abstract from the literary form?

This latter has, time and again, been maintained in writings about Plato. For Wilamowitz,[4] for example, the understanding of Plato's philosophy requires "that poetry be treated as poetry." Of course, this depends on what one means by "poetry." Is it merely the imagination's playing with forms? Or is it a particular way of grasping reality? Also in Hegel's lectures on the history of philosophy,[5] there is a telling comment which, precisely by virtue of its being a *passing* comment, shows how much he can take for granted the thought expressed in it. Hegel speaks of a seemingly lost writing of Plato. The loss is especially regrettable because it was probably not a dialogue but a "purely philosophical work," a "dogmatic," essentially didactic piece: "so what we are left with is only his dialogues." Does this mean that the dialogue form and any kind of story is not a "pure" form of philosophical utterance? This was undoubtedly Hegel's view. He has expressed it on many occasions: "the only true form in which truth exists" is "the scientific (philosophical) system."[6]

But is it really true that the "dogmatic" sentence expressed in general concepts is quite simply the best for attaining truth? Of course, the question, "Who is my neighbor," can be answered with a definition; but whether it is more correct or more true than the story with which the New Testament answers and which begins with the words, "A man was going from Jerusalem to Jericho and fell among thieves,"[7] may reasonably be doubted. Moreover, could it not be the case that the reality most relevant to man is not a "set of facts" but is rather an "event," and that it accordingly cannot be grasped adequately in a thesis but only, to use Aristotle's words, in a *präxeos mímesis*,[8] in the representation of an action – in other words, in a story?

These are the kinds – and this is their importance – of questions one has to deal with when investigating the meaning above all of the *mythical* stories found in Plato's works. Of course, the word "myth" refers to a particular kind of story which covers only a small part of what Plato has his characters relate in the dialogues. But what is a myth? Even the attempt to give a purely formal definition of the concept brings into play the fundamentally diverging views which concern the structure of reality as a whole – especially since, in the case of the word "myth," common Greek usage as well as that of Plato and modern Greek is extremely differentiated, even Babylonian, and seems at first sight to pave the way for every conceivable definition.

According to the dictionaries[9] the word "myth," in common Greek usage, can have a confusingly varied number of meanings: word, speech, conversations, proverb; it can even mean the word that is merely thought and not yet spoken, the plan, the sketch. Of course, there is also the narrower meaning: story, narrative, saga, fairytale; possibly, even preferably, the invented "untrue" story. Correspondingly, there are the many related words like *mythéomai* and *mythologéo*: I speak, I say; I recount or invent a story. – The English equivalent of *mythologia* is given as "fiction": a fabricated occurrence, the narration of an invented story. – It seems that such wide diversity is found in all languages, precisely in the word field of "speaking." Saga, for instance, taken literally, means no more than "that which one says"; but in fact, in the living language there are connotations of what is prehistory and even what has a dubious relation to historical truth. Or, the most obvious meaning of the word "story" is, admittedly, simply that some event is recounted; but if I ask someone if he is "telling me a story" I am asking if he is not spinning me a yarn. We encounter precisely this usage also in the Platonic dialogues. When Socrates is on the point of telling the unreceptive powerful pragmatist, Callicles, the myth about judgment after death, he makes it clear how few illusions he has about the probable reaction of his listener: "You will, of course, take this to be a story [*mythos*]; but I take it to be truth."[10]

It is therefore clear that one has to be ready for complications even when one is investigating Platonic use of language. If one attempts to draw up a summary catalogue of the meanings of the word *mythos* in Plato's writings, the result is as follows: "myths" are in the first instance the fairytales one tells to children; there is some truth in them, but they are not really true.[11] According to what we read in a late dialogue,[12] the notions of the early philosophers about the making of the universe strike us as being of this kind: "Myths they tell us as if we were children." – Socrates tells us a quite different kind of story when it is a question of the origin of tyranny;[13] although it is not meant to be taken literally, it is true and valid in its own eerie way. Socrates asks Adeimantus: "Have you never heard the story [*mython*] that anyone who has tasted human flesh and blood – for instance, mixed in with that of sacrificial animals – inevitably turns into a wolf?" And when Adeimantus says he has, Socrates continues, asking whether it is not the same for those who have political power: "when he has defiled himself with blood on his hands, when his godless mouth has tasted the murder of human being, does he not inevitably fall victim to the disaster of turning into a tyrant and, from being a man, become a wolf?"

Different again are the stories, which Plato also calls "myths" – about the prehistoric foundation of states, about the origin of customs and constitutions of the various peoples – according to which they are the result of divine decree. This brings us closer to the central area of meaning where "myth," in the strict sense of the word, resides. Here there are the stories of the genesis of the cosmos, the primeval stories of salvation and destruction of mankind, the fate of the dead, judgment, and punishment in the other life.

A reader who, full of astonishment, has become acquainted with the beginning of Plato's *Republic*, would very soon – even before discussion about the state commences – find mention of such myths.[14] Socrates has gone into the house of his friends and finds in the atrium old Cephalus, still adorned after coming from attending a sacrifice. He sits down with him: "I like talking with men advanced in years; they have made a journey which we, too, have to make. So I would like to hear from you your thoughts on what the poets call 'the threshold of old age . . .'" Cephalus gives him a lengthy answer. Then he says this: "When the time approaches where a man preoccupies himself with the thought of death, worry arises about things which previously have caused him little concern. Thus the myths that are told about our fate in the underworld, that anyone who has committed crimes here must be punished for them in the other world – these stories which one has previously laughed about make one uneasy: they could, in the end, be true . . ."

Here, also for Plato himself, the question of truth is of particular importance. More precisely, he has always attributed to stories which are in the strict sense mythical an incomparably valid truth, a truth which, in a completely unique way is inviolable and beyond all doubt; although, on the other hand, it always remained a concrete question for him as to how the message of the myth could be converted into human speech and not be lost.[15] But this is a new theme which is later to be dealt with explicitly.

As will already have become clear, stories which are in the proper sense mythical are played out between "here" and "beyond," between the realms of the divine and the human. They deal with the activity of the gods insofar as it affects human beings, and with the activity of human beings insofar as it engages with the gods. This characteristic is largely confirmed by established word usage in the history of religion, in ethnology, and in the general history of ideas. "Myth is divine history. That is *the* definition of the word, which must not be abandoned" – according to Paul Tillich, who also adds that "what we are dealing with here is not a literary, but rather a religious category."[16]

With this definition, however, the concept of myth is not completely delineated. A further element is found in the shortcomings of speech – the impossibility of giving adequate expression in speech to what is contained in the concept. If one were to take a mythical story literally – for instance, if one were to read the myth of the judgment of the dead on the sacred meadow at the underworld crossroads[17] as an official record of criminal proceedings, one would have fundamentally misunderstood what was really meant. The events take place outside the historical world that we can understand – beyond the here and now. For this reason it is only possible to use the language of symbol[18] – not for the sake of some kind of literary device but because there is no other possibility.

That is, by the way, yet another reason why the myths told by Plato have to appear, from the position of rationalist system thinking, as an inadequate kind of philosophical statement justified only by the impossibility "of giving purer accounts of the thought" – which is another quotation from Hegel.[19] His judgment in this matter has for a long time been a decisive influence in interpreting Plato. For example, in Eduard Zeller's great historical work we read: "Plato's myths point . . . almost always to a gap in scientific (philosophical) knowledge."[20] – Plato himself would basically agree with this. Socrates, too, showed a certain understanding for those who felt the myth of the judgment of the dead had no meaning for them.[21] He said that at least there was nothing surprising in such a refusal – *if* we were in a position, through careful investigation, to discover something better and truer. You are right, he says, symbolic speech is a makeshift. It is not the real way to express the truth. But what if the real way is not available to us? This is the situation we find ourselves in. "It is difficult, my friend, to express higher things without recourse to sense images. In this we are like the person who knows everything in a dream and in waking no longer knows anything."[22]

Almost more important than the elements of the concept of myth mentioned so far is the third element: that the narrator of the myth is, explicitly, not its author. It is accepted that the myths related by Plato derive neither from himself nor from Socrates. This negative fact can be proven with complete clarity. Not only do Socrates and Plato never make any claim to such authorship, they also leave no room for doubt that they themselves have been recipients of what they are reporting and that they do not consider themselves empowered to add anything to the myth or to subtract anything from it. Naturally, Plato uses his own words. But he sees himself as one who reports a story. He does not speak as an eyewitness but as one who passes on what has been handed down. And even when his communication, as is only to be expected, bears the stamp of his own inspired language, it still remains clear that the messenger is not the author of the message to be handed down.

As we have seen, that is, in the first instance, only a negative assertion, yet it has some important consequences. For instance, it immediately disqualifies what has become the normally accepted view that Plato, with his original literary genius and "conscious art,"[23] "created" those mythical stories, "because through them he could express his metaphysical ideas better, more easily, and more forcefully."[24]

On the other hand, if Plato is only reporting the myths found in his dialogues, the unavoidable question is: who, then, is the real author? This question clearly implies the further question of how myth is legitimized; what is the basis for its being believed; how is it "authenticated"? Can it be authenticated at all? The German dictionary of the brothers Grimm is not able to say much more about myth than that it is "an *un*authenticated story."[25] For the time being I would like to view that as a rather dubious if not simply wrong answer. Of course, what kind of authentication of a myth would be possible? The answer to this question depends on who is considered to be the real, original author of the myth.

II

THE CONCEPT OF MYTH IN THE STRICT SENSE APPLIES TO
an unexpectedly small sector of the broad and colorful field of Platonic stories. It does not even include all stories about the gods. When Phaedrus
asks him whether he believes the legend of the ab-
duction of the nymph Oreithyia by Boreas,
Socrates answers that he has not yet thought
about it; "I don't even have enough time to satisfy
the Delphic oracle that says to me: Know thy-
self!"[1] On occasions this dismissive indifference
with regard to a local allegorical saga has been interpreted[2] as an expression of Plato's fundamental
attitude toward myth as such. In reality, it seems
to me that precisely here the contrast to his completely un-ironic seriousness in considering gen-
uinely mythical truth is revealed. – Even the story
that Iris, the messenger of the gods, is a daughter
of Thaumas,[3] is in no way a myth for Plato. On the
contrary, he sees it as nothing more than a comment illustrating the thought that the philosophical act springs from astonishment [thaumázein].

Furthermore, Diotima's story of the procreation of Zeus from the embrace of Poros and Penia, of wealth and poverty,[4] is clearly, if only through being a personification of the abstract, the opposite of symbolic and therefore mythical speech: the concept is, as expressed in Goethe's accurate definition of allegory,[5] "to be found in the image," while the idea expressed symbolically, although having an unending influence through the image, can neither be grasped nor expressed in it.

Everything that in Plato literature passes for "allegorical myths"[6] is therefore excluded from our study, as is also everything that may be attributed to the literary Plato as "artistic myth."[7] It is simply an inauthentic use of words to refer to the *Republic* as a whole or any other Platonic dialogue as a myth. And the story in *Gorgias*[8] of the helmsman (after he has performed the great feat of bringing people, the man with wife and child, in safety over the sea to the Piraeus, "he disembarks from the boat and walks in his simple clothes along the shore and is able to say he is not sure whom he has helped or harmed") – these masterly ten lines are no more to be understood as myth than are the innumerable parables and images which are to be found in almost all the dialogues: the soul of the licentious is a leaky container into which the wretched souls scoop water with a sieve;[9] the poet is like a magnet that communicates its own energy to the iron, so that those inspired by the muse propagate their inspiration to others, and a whole chain of inspired ones is attached to them;[10] the mind of man is a wax tablet into which, as with a signet ring, memory is pressed[11] – and so forth. Even the parable of the cave, the most cited of all of Plato's myths, is not a myth in the strict sense, although it has been called that thousands of times. Not only are there no gods involved, nor does the action take place between the divine and the human spheres; the whole of it is – and here there is no dispute – written in the clef "as if" ("Would the incarcerated, if they could speak to one another, not agree to give the shadows specific names?"[12]). But the parable, exactly as with the story of the ring of Gyges in the *Republic*, clearly serves to illustrate something that lies outside the story itself; this something is what is actually important and real. By contrast, the strictly mythical story does not merely report on something which is undoubtedly real. It does not refer to anything else; it concerns itself exclusively with something expressed directly *in* the story itself – no matter how unattainable and unfathomable this may be for human reason.

Which stories in Plato's work are mythical in the strict sense? What stands apart in this mixture of stories? The following: the story told in the *Timaeus* about the creation of the world; the report hidden in Aristophanes' speech in the *Symposium* about man in his original state and about his fall; above all, the eschatological myths placed at the end of *Gorgias*, the *Republic*, and *Phaedo* about the other world, about judgment, and about the fate of the dead.

Of course, it must be said that a sprinkling of fragments of genuine myths is to be found in the soil of almost all Platonic dialogues, embedded in the argument. For example, in the early dialogue *Crito*, written down at a time when it seems Plato had as yet no sense for the mythical,[13] suddenly we read: "Value nothing higher than justice so that in the underworld you can use it in your defense before those who rule there."[14] – Another embedded fragment is found at the beginning of the *Phaedo*. The question is raised: why should it not be allowed to take one's own life if death is such a good thing? Socrates answers by using the mythical tradition: "What is taught in the mysteries seems to me very significant, namely, that we human beings are like sentries and are not allowed to leave our post of our own volition; the other point that is made also seems right to me: that the gods are our guardians and that we (men) are one of the flocks belonging to the gods."[15] Socrates says that, of course, he does not know this of himself but from what he has heard, *ex akoés*. The German Plato translations[16] say without exception "vom Hörensagen" (from hearsay). It is clear that the original meaning is thereby not only obscured but even misrepresented. The same combination of words recurs in another Greek text, some centuries after Plato, in St. Paul's Epistle to the *Romans* [10, 17]: "Faith comes from hearing" [*ex akoés*]. The meaning is the same as in *Phaedo*: that something one has not seen oneself or does not already know is accepted as true on the word of someone else.

But not only is the reasoning and discursive argumentation of the dialogues continually interrupted by a sprinkling of mythical fragments, but inversely, the flow of the myths – told with coherence and, as it were, all in one breath – is for its part often impeded by the presence of foreign elements which are clearly non-mythical in character. This impurity, this inclusion of elements which do not belong, this crusting over with fantastic accessories which can make the essential communication indecipherable – all this, it seems, is unavoidable. It is essentially bound up with the inner situation of the narrator himself. This is especially the case in the more important matter, that, quite apart from such a mixture, everything mythical is by its very nature a *fragment*. The great mythical stories, they too, are only fragments of a tradition which Plato can no longer grasp as a whole – no longer, or not yet. He seems to have sensed that himself. This is seen in the occasional comments found, for example, in a late dialogue,[17] where it is said that with the passing of the ages parts of the wonderful old stories have been completely erased, other parts have been scattered far and wide, and individual parts have been separated from the whole – and no one is able to give the reason. On the other hand it has been said of Plato[18] that his achievement consists precisely in his being able "to purify fragments of a . . . great myth, to join them, and to give them a new shape." I am convinced that Plato was precisely *not* in a position to achieve this very thing. Faced with the whole body of mythical tradition that lay before him, he was not able to distinguish the true from the false, the kernel from the shell, the essential from the secondary. This is where *pre*-Christian thinking encounters an insurmountable barrier.

The Platonic Myths

It is clear that at this point fundamentally divergent views again come into play – and, indeed, as I see it, unavoidably. In no way does the question of truth here find expression all of a sudden – as a kind of short-circuited view of the world. It is easy to show that it has been constantly under discussion for a long time. For example, it is inevitable that the eschatological myths related by Plato mean something entirely different to the modern interpreter – depending on whether he believes that there really is a judgment after death or whether he thinks such a belief is absurd. In the first case it would not occur to him, vis-à-vis the myth about the other world narrated in *Gorgias*, to speak of "fantastic notions" or even of "highly absurd inventions";[19] he will probably also not call this myth a "fairytale"[20] that is merely "playful" and in no way to be taken seriously.[21] But, as is well known, such formulations are not at all uncommon in scholarly Plato literature. That these are – even purely as text interpretation – grotesquely false can often enough be shown by an analysis which looks carefully at individual detail. But naturally one arrives at that fundamental underlying conviction, whatever it is, not on the basis of Plato studies. Whoever accepts as truth the kernel of the great myths recounted by Plato can only do so, just as Socrates did, *ex akoés*, by listening to that same voice that must also have reached ear of Plato himself.

III

THE PLATONIC DIALOGUES SELDOM FINISH WITH AN actual conclusion. Normally they do not produce anything that could be formulated as a "well-rounded truth"[1] but rather the insight that the secret of the world cannot be grasped in this particular way. So the conversations end precisely with the thinker facing into the unforeseeable. – Yet there are three great dialogues which do not fit this pattern: *Gorgias*, *Republic*, and *Phaedo*. These dialogues do not end with an open question but with a conclusion – which, admittedly, in all three cases, is a myth. The theme is in each case the same: the *éschata*, the "last things" of mankind.

Plato was thirty-five years old when he wrote *Gorgias*. This is the first time that he openly says what he thinks of the truth of myths.[2] The fate of the dead obviously fascinated the philosopher throughout his life. As has rightly been said,[3] there is hardly one of the dialogues to which the realm of death is closed. It is through Plato that the consideration of death became an integral part of the definition of philosophy. There is no reason for surprise that *Phaedo*, the great conversation between friends in Socrates' death cell, ends with an eschatological myth. But that *Gorgias* and the *Republic*, both of them completely concerned with the order in which our shared historical existence is played out, should also end in a myth about the other world – that is not at all immediately obvious. And it would be worth the trouble to inquire about the "linkup,"[4] about the thought-joint by which in these dialogues the mythical narration and the rational argumentation are bound together.

In *Gorgias*, Socrates tries, in an attempt that is doomed to failure from the beginning, to convince Callicles, a cynical pragmatist interested only in power, that to commit an injustice is worse than to suffer an injustice, and that it is worthwhile to be just even though it might mean thereby risking one's life. To this Callicles replies: And so you think it is all right for a man not to know how to look after himself?[5] Yes, Socrates answers, I do find that is acceptable, insofar as the man has already looked after himself – by staying away from injustice in the eyes of gods and men, in words and deeds. Then Socrates, ironically but in complete seriousness, takes over the categories of the man interested in power, saying: such a man is truly successful, strong, on top, and has asserted himself, whereas real helplessness and failure as such lies in going down to Hades laden down with one's injustice: "If you like, I will tell you an old story about this."[6]

And so the first Platonic myth is told to deaf ears, beginning with the tragically paradoxical request: "Then hear . . ."[7] That is, as Socrates himself says, the traditional formula, the significance of which of course should not be over-interpreted. At the same time, this important term "hear" is deliberately put at the beginning. And it recurs at the end: "This, Callicles, is what I have *heard* and what I believe to be the truth."[8] Between such a beginning and such an end there is the lengthy story about a tribunal judging the dead, about its functioning, and about its history. Socrates (Plato) himself gives an interpretation which he inserts into the simple narration identifying what he thinks is fundamental (this, too, is a non-mythical – expressed positively, a *theological* element – insofar as theology can be defined as the attempt to interpret sacred tradition). The kernel of the mythical story is the following: wrongdoing is not over and done with as soon as the act has been committed. On the contrary, something remains in the soul, like the scar of a wound, even after death. This does not escape the unerring gaze of the judge, who pronounces a correct and unwavering judgment and apportions reward or punishment. The reward is to dwell on the islands of the blessed. Punishment, like guilt, is in two forms. The guilty who can be healed are led to a place at which, for a time, they "do penance" and "purify themselves of their wrongdoing."[9] And so, when we speak of a "place of purification" and "purgatory" we are using Plato's own words. Those who through their crime have incurred guilt which cannot be healed undergo – as a warning spectacle to those who do wrong – an unending, eternal punishment, *eis aeí chronon*[10] (Schleiermacher translates this: "für ewige Zeit" [for time eternal]). This, then, reduced to its simplest form, is the mythical truth which interests Socrates (and Plato).

(This mythical truth) is seen in all its clarity when compared with Homer's ideas of the afterlife. Here there is no hint of a justice that rewards and punishes and once and for all passes judgment on the world of human beings.[11] Among the shades that Odysseus sees when he conjures up the dead, that band of ghostly monsters which greedily press forward to the puddle of black blood that drips from the slaughtered sacrificial animals onto the ground and which Odysseus drives back with his sword – among them is Achilles, the hero of Homer's song. The encounter with him that is now described amounts to a destruction of faith. When Odysseus sees him he tells Achilles he is lucky, while he himself is still wretched and dogged by misfortune: "For when you were alive we honored you as one of the gods / All Achaeans did. And here you are the ruler among the dead." Achilles replies with words which, in the mouth of a prince, are devastating:[12] "Don't praise death to me, illustrious Odysseus. If only I were a servant doing forced labor in the fields, in the service of an impoverished man, instead of being, down here, king in the realm of the dead."[13] In the *Republic*[14] there are utterances which show how deeply affected Plato must have been by this information gleaned from Homer – not only for its hopelessness but also because of its being a fundamental untruth.

His own conviction about life after death is not yet fully expressed in the *Gorgias* myth. The myths related at the end of *Republic* and of *Phaedo* add something new to the picture – although basically all three myths say the same thing. This is, of course, to a large extent contested. According to Couturat's book, *De mythis Platonicis*,[15] these are three completely different stories, and precisely their difference proves that they are not meant as "truth" and that accordingly Plato has here no conviction that should be taken seriously. It is, in fact, true that in *Phaedo*, instead of the "islands of the blessed" he speaks of the "true earth" and in *Republic* he speaks of "heaven"; and also the punishments in the afterlife are described differently. But precisely this belongs to the nature of all symbolic speech: because the real truth to be communicated is beyond the realm of our experience it can be expressed in a variety of sense images, none of which can lay claim, in its detail, to being the simply authentic one. Because the "heavenly realm" is beyond our experience we need to have it said, in various ways, what it "resembles": a banquet, a wedding, a treasure buried in a field, a fishing net, a mustard seed, a [day of] reckoning – and so on. The only important thing is the one aspect that all of these symbols express. Even in the eschatological myths related by Plato the variety of material is not what counts but the single identical *forma* that carries the meaning, namely, that the existence of man is such that its ultimate success (and also its ultimate failure) is only revealed "beyond" [*ekéi*). However, the eschatological myths recounted later introduce individual new elements – for example, the idea of the daimonic companion who is already allotted to man in his earthly life and who also, after death, leads him to the place of judgment in the other world.[16] Furthermore, there is mention, in each of the three eschatological myths, of a temporal punishment, a kind of purification. One of them, however, adds a further detail, according to which, with uncanny consistency, the idea is presented that human beings are a community which survives death: those, namely, who are sent to the place of purification would be rid of their punishment on condition that they are expressly forgiven by those whom they have wronged.[17] But above all in the *Phaedo* myth there is a new, moving element characterizing the place of the blessed. What is special about this "pure dwelling"[18] is that in the temples and shrines there are not just images of the gods, but the gods themselves in truth live there,[19] so that a real *synousia*, a companionship of gods and men, comes about.

Of course, the later eschatological stories add non-mythical elements as well – to such an extent that one could almost speak of a crusting over of the real myth by secondary non-mythical elements. Whoever naively reads the myth about the afterlife in *Phaedo* could easily be led to believe that it deals with a theory of the construction of the earth – with its surface shape as well as the structure beneath the surface, with its underground water courses, etc. Such utterances do, in fact, make up by far the greatest part of the story. But one has to realize that the real assimilation of mythical truth necessarily demands that one think of what is *believed* and what is *known* at one and the same time. Anyone who seriously undertakes to interpret as truth something that has been handed down cannot simply leave aside his "natural" acquired knowledge of the world and of men. Today, no theologian who tries to interpret the biblical account of creation can dispense with an extremely close examination of the findings of research in the fields of paleontology and evolution, so it is not surprising that Plato tries to link contemporary knowledge of the earth's structure with the mythical notions of the other world. And the commentator who sees Plato's description linking the circulation of water on earth with the underworld and the other underground water courses as an "Essay on a Theory of Hydrography"[20] is not altogether wrong. Naturally we reach a cul-de-sac when in the same breath – with regard to this admittedly inadequate theory which is nevertheless an attempt at being scientific – he dismisses as phantasmagoric[21] Plato's description of the "true earth" as a place where the blessed dwell.

The hopeless aspect of such rationalism is that anything that is not a "scientific statement" is considered to be purely fanciful; no third possibility is seen that is neither one nor the other – for example, myth. There is no doubt that Plato, both in *Phaedo* and in *Republic*, took very seriously the cosmological theories linked with the telling of the myth. However, for the myth as a whole they are not decisive, not even for Plato himself. They belong to the description of the "housing" in which the decisive element takes place. Also in Dante's poem depicting the world, a whole theory of the cosmos and the concentric circles in which the heavenly bodies move is developed. Of this, too, it is true to say that it is not the essential thing but a description of the "housing" in which the essential takes place. Who would seriously maintain that the core poetic – and mythical – statement in the *Divine Comedy* is at all affected by the modern correction of medieval cosmology! In exactly the same way it is not possible to affect the core statement in Plato's myths about the afterlife by totally rejecting the material shell. Plato himself would immediately abandon this without giving up one iota of the mythical truth, which, right through the epochs of human history, always says the same thing: namely, that the real result of our earthly existence is manifested on the other side of death in an event which, in symbolical language, is called "judgment of the dead." This event is not accessible to our imagination; it is not something we can experience. It takes place between the divine and human sphere, outside of historical time.

IV

"The last things" – the future that is beyond our experience – and also the origin of the world and of mankind – these can only be grasped in information that, while not the result of experience and thinking, is able, however, in a unique way to throw light on and open up for us both experience and thought. In Plato's work there are two mythical stories which go right back to the past that precedes all the known history of mankind. One of them focuses on man, and the other on the cosmos as a whole.

The myth concerning the primeval fate of man is formulated in a strange, irregular, and illogical way: in Aristophanes' speech in the *Symposium*. Its seriousness is almost all too successfully obscured behind the mask of the writer of comedy. Try to imagine for a moment that the original version of the biblical account of paradise has been lost and has survived only as parody in a Shakespearean comedy or, even worse, in the form of a farce by James Thurber. You are faced with the task of interpreting this scarcely decipherable text to find the serious meaning hidden in it. One is faced with a similar difficulty when one undertakes to interpret Aristophanes' speech in the *Symposium*. And so it is only to be expected that in the literature about Plato not only extremely varied but even diametrically opposed interpretations are to be found. Some speak of the marvelous joke, the charming game;[1] the whole is referred to as a *vere comica oratio* and a *ridicula fibula*.[2] For others it is at least a poetic piece created "with all the means that fantasy has at its disposal."[3] There is also an interpretation according to which this piece of comedy has "the paradoxical quality of being tragic";[4] it should be understood as a downright theological utterance expressing the deepest existential seriousness.[5] And it is clear that anyone who speaks of a mythical core to Aristophanes' speech is not all that far away from this last conception.

Without keeping in mind the situation of the *Symposium*, it is not possible to understand this speech, its inner style and tonality. The guests of the fashionable successful writer Agathon, gathered together to celebrate a newly awarded prize for literature, have decided on the spur of the moment that everyone present should, *ex tempore*, make a speech about Eros. The climate of this gathering is spiced, moreover, with very different kinds of ingredients: a relaxed mood, exhilaration, contempt for the trivial, elation, and a quite unceremonious seriousness are all part of it. Before Aristophanes speaks, several others have already made their contributions. Enthusiasm and emotional involvement, rationally superior approach to living, aesthetically cultivated sensuality; psychology, sociology, biology – all that has had its say. Aristophanes is the first to enter the dimension of the mythical, saying that before being able to say what the real meaning of Eros is one would have to know about human nature and human experience, the *pathémata*[6] of man; one would have to consider what has happened to us in relation to the gods in our pre-historical time. And he immediately begins with the mythical story of our original state and of the fall of man. In talking this way he constantly makes lightning-quick changes of register – to the amusement, but also to the confusion, both of his audience and of later readers of Plato. The dignified communication of wisdom is constantly and without warning interrupted by burlesque and peals of laughter.

But since we are not concerned here with Aristophanes himself nor even with Plato's

Symposium, nor with the essence of Eros, let us inquire directly about the elements of the mythical story itself which Plato tells in such a complicated way. What is said about man's past and the things that happened to him, about these things beyond our experience, beyond the threshold of our self-understanding? This is what is said:[7] Formerly, *pálai*, in the beginning ("in paradise") man was a completely perfect being; he had the shape of a sphere, which in antiquity was "the most perfect of all forms."[8] In a word, human nature was sound and unscathed. But "now," in our historical time it is "totally different"; man's nature is determined by the loss of that original wholeness. This loss has been imposed as a divine punishment, after men, bewitched by their own "great thoughts," tried to force their way into heaven and to rise up against the gods. This is when man had his original perfection taken from him. He was cut into two halves – "as one cuts an egg into pieces with a horse-hair."[9]

At this point I am unable to resist the temptation to introduce a polemical digression: about the nonsense of an "interpretation" based purely on material elements and what they have generated. The term "egg," for example, has sparked off a real hunt for every other mention of eggs in the myths of the nations. Thus the egg-shaped *materia prima* – part of the orphic teaching of the genesis of the world – and also the legendary twins deriving from a silver egg, have been cited.[10] Does one need to say explicitly that of course this brings nothing at all to the understanding of Plato's story? Such learned nonsense recalls to mind the footnote which an enthusiastic commentator added to one of Goethe's "Aphorisms in Prose." According to the aphorism: "Hindus in the desert vow not to eat fish";[11] the footnote, in which a Greek text is quoted, offers for consideration that Pythagoras also forbade "the eating of fish."[12] If instead of this one had noted that the poachers in the Lüneburger Heide take an oath not to shoot antelopes one would have remained closer to the point than with such a purely material pseudo-analogy. In a word, whether it is to do with Goethe or Plato, the material elements – apart from the *forma* imprinted on them – mean nothing.

The loss of the original whole form – as the Aristophanes myth goes on to say – did not affect only those who were guilty; no, "*we*, because of our injustice have been cut in pieces by God."[13] This is not just a question of guilt, but of *hereditary* guilt. Historical man is the heir to crime committed before our history began and to the loss incurred as a punishment. His earthly existence is, in Plato's view, deeply affected and molded by fate – as it is called in the mythical story – in the distant past and outside of human experience; so much so that, without this knowledge, man would not only be incomprehensible to himself (for example, in regard to the "real" significance of the emotional turmoil experienced through eros), but he might not even be capable of living an authentic human life.

Still more deeply than the Aristophanes speech in the *Symposium*, the *Timaeus* dialogue delves into the origins which lie beyond all our experience. It deals with the absolute beginning not of man but of the world as a whole. Anyone who, in this context, uses the term "world creation" in the sense that has become customary in Plato literature must realize that neither Plato nor any other thinker in antiquity – outside of the biblical tradition – used the term "creation" in the exact and strict sense, not even, so it seems, in interpreting the sacred tradition. Naturally, one should not forget that the idea of *creatio*, the complete positing of being independently of anything from which it derived, cannot be adequately grasped. Even when we say "production *from* nothing" inevitably a false image comes into play: that of the nothing *out of* which things were made. However, it can justifiably be said that Plato was convinced that the cosmos and all being as such was the work of God's activity. For him that is simply an incontrovertible truth. "All mortal beings, everything on the earth that grows from seed or root, and also all lifeless things – whether such as melt or do not melt – that are formed in the earth": all of these things come about through "the demiurgic force of God" and "through the art of God";[14] they are, without exception, "works of divine origin."[15] "We know that we ourselves and other living things, as well as what constitutes everything that has come into being – fire and water and such like – , are produced by God."[16] All of these statements, none of which, by the way, occurs in the context of a mythical story, are taken from the *Sophist* dialogue. Plato wrote it when he was an old man. The *Timaeus* dialogue belongs to the same period. It is an exception in that, as a whole, it can be called one single big mythical story – though it is strewn with innumerable fragments of a non-mythical character. No work of Plato is so confusing as the *Timaeus*. On its journeys along its tangled routes it is constantly stopping and changing direction. The elements and their proportions are described; it deals with the course of the stars and how the concepts of number and time are related; a theory of space is outlined; there is talk of the functions and structure of the human body as well as of a possible classification of man's sicknesses; there is discussion of the origin of animals – and so on and so forth. It is astounding how clearly the myth of the birth of the cosmos emerges – out of this confused and colorful tapestry – as a very simply organized structure. Its statement can be reduced to a few sentences. The first is that there is "a maker and father of all this";[17] sometimes he is referred to as the "founder" or "regulator";[18] sometimes as the "procreating Father."[19] Furthermore, the cosmos is necessarily, of its very nature, an *eikón*, a reproduction of something[20] – something that never changes in itself[21] and that is eternal.[22] But the middle of the *Timaeus* myth is made up of a series of sentences which need to be quoted *verbatim*: "So we want to state why the founder *did* found all that has come into being and the totality of the world: *because he is good*. But the good person knows no kind of malevolence because of anything or against anyone. So, free from any kind of jealousy, he wanted everything to be as like him as possible. This, above all, is the highest origin of the world and its becoming – just as wise men also call him the most understanding. Therefore, because God wanted everything, so far as possible, to be good and nothing to be bad, he brought everything out of disorder into order."[23] The mythical statement about the world closes with the sentence that reality is and remains *one* world because of such an origin.[24]

Pausing at this point one can look back on the *corpus* of myths recounted in Plato's work. Not only is one surprised at the simplicity and unity of Plato's view of the world – which emerges despite the confusing variety in the material – but one is also struck by the unexpected accord between this view and the teachings and stories which Christianity also has always cherished and revered as true. What is astounding, above all, is that the conception of the beginning of the world and the final perfection of man is almost identical. For Plato, just as for the Christian, it is from the ungrudging goodness of the Creator that everything has its origin. And who would want to make a distinction between, on the one hand, Plato's speech about the life of the blessed being shared with the gods themselves[25] – and not just with their images – and, on the other hand, the mention of God's "tent among men" and that "God himself dwells among them"?[26] Who would, if he did not know already it, hit on the idea that these last two texts are taken not from Plato's *Phaedo* but from the New Testament?

V

ANYONE WHO THINKS OF ASKING WHAT PLATO HIMSELF thought about the *truth* of the myths he relates will soon realize that he has thereby entered an arena and where he is no longer in a position *not* to do battle. While one should think it possible to answer this question fairly reliably with methods of careful, clean-cut interpretation, the reality is that there is an almost Babylonian multiplicity of the most different opinions. This is clearly linked with the fact that the very choice of myths to be studied is usually influenced by quite fundamental pre-formed convictions. In such a case, it is necessary and helpful to do two things: to "declare" as clearly as possible – as when crossing the border – one's own ultimate opinions and also to show the justification for them in each text being considered.

According to my thesis, then, Plato held that the meaning contained in the myths is inviolable truth. – Perhaps it is worth saying a word here about what is meant by "truth." The examination question occasionally asked by logicians is familiar: when is the sentence "men live on Mars" true? The answer expected is that the sentence is true when men do live on Mars. In this simple example the meaning is expressed with complete clarity. The Platonic myths about the beginning of the world and the "last things," about the divine origin of the world, about the perfection of man's nature in paradise and the loss of it, about judgment after death – these stories are true if such things happen. And precisely this, I maintain, is Plato's conviction.

The first counter-argument goes way beyond the theme "Plato's myths." Karl Reinhardt has put it in a nutshell. Shortly before he died I was, by chance, his neighbor at table at a congress meal. I asked him whether he still held the view expressed in his little book – published decades earlier[1] – that all these stories were merely thought-games which Plato himself did not at all take seriously. After a brief hesitation he answered quite emphatically: "There is no such thing as faith for the ancient Greeks!"[2] Karl Reinhardt is, of course, by no means alone in making this assumption. "The heathens . . . had no articles of faith," says Leibniz;[3] and in Überweg's history, incidentally in the chapter on Plato's *Timaeus*, it says one should not be looking for exact statements of dogma from the myths."[4] From another angle – that of the modern history of religion – this has been energetically repeated using respectable material presented by scholars: "Man in antiquity . . . never felt bound to see mythical stories . . . as historical reality. He never affirmed them. Myth had nothing in common with a belief in the sense of 'holding something to be true.' . . . Myth in heathen antiquity was to some extent open. It was not under any authority which officially promulgated and watched over it."[5]

It is worthwhile looking more closely at individual points of this text just quoted. – First, it seems to me possible to see something as true without taking it to be *historical reality*. For example, the Christian believer does not look on the biblical account of creation or the story of paradise as historical reality, and yet he is convinced that there is some element of inviolable truth in these stories. Second, it is unquestionable that for man in ancient times myths were not subject to any authority – insofar as one means by "authority" an official teaching institution. But that does not at all mean that the myths are simply "open" to manipulation by just any arbiter.

When, for example, Plato[6] says "it is fitting to

give credence to the old and sacred words telling us that the soul is immortal and will come before the judge," it is clear that he is speaking of an authority whose mode of existence and whose binding character are, of course, difficult to grasp. Whatever about the beliefs of the ancients in general or of the ancient Greeks as a whole: at least for Plato it can be shown that he accepts myth as a form of truth and that he believed in that truth. And if he, as is hardly likely, is an exception, then he is an exception of considerable weight.

Perhaps the previously used formulation – that in the Plato literature there is, in this regard, a Babylonian multiplicity of opinions – may strike some as exaggerated. For this reason it is good to speak very concretely and to see what interpretations have been given to a particular text. Let the text be a sentence from the *Timafeus*. The theme is the one we have been talking about. *Timaeus* recounts the myth of the creation of the world and says: "Because it is beyond our capacity to speak of divine things, we have to believe those who have brought tidings of them and can call themselves descendants of the gods and therefore have certain knowledge handed down to them from their ancestors. It is not permitted us to refuse credence to the sons of the gods even if what they teach is neither likely nor demonstrable."[7] The question is what this sentence means. In Plato literature the following answers are given:[8]

1. The statement is to be understood as the true expression of the devout acceptance of sacred tradition that characterizes the late Plato;[9]
2. The sentence is, so to speak, a tactical gesture on Plato's part, explained by his worry that, like Socrates, he could be charged with godlessness;[10]
3. It is conceivable that the words could have been meant ironically;[11]
4. This is not only possible but is in fact the case. It is "a deep irony that goes as far as mockery" (this interpretation derives from Eduard Zeller, Hegel's pupil[12]).

Who is right? Naturally this can only be decided on the basis of an understanding which takes account of the whole *Timaeus* dialogue and which then, of course, has to find its own justification in the details of the text itself.

And also, with regard to the basic opinions by which such an interpretation is inevitably influenced, it is not as though – despite the fundamental impossibility of proof – they are incapable of critical justification.

But we are still engaged in considering the counter–arguments, which seem to say that Plato, or Socrates as well, did not accept the myths as truth. For example, how otherwise – so the argument goes – are we to understand that Socrates, straight after recounting the myth about the beyond – seemingly with extreme seriousness as one preparing himself for death, and deeply moved by his own narration – should immediately and expressly call it into question? Clearly, at the end he does not shrink from "shattering the certainty of the myth again."[13] And does it not emerge in all clarity that in Plato's view, generally, what we have here is "not *Aletheia* but *Pseudos*"?[14] Also, this interpretation, which is virtually the prevailing one, often enough influences the translation. And it would be worth taking the trouble to search through the most widely known German Plato editions to see what happens to a basic word like *mythos*.[15] The worst thing about such touch-ups is that the distortion of the overall picture is hardly noticed and for that reason can scarcely be corrected.

What, then, is the significance of the supposed retraction of the myth in *Phaedo*? – Socrates finished the story about the reward of the blessed with a word of confirmation meant for himself and his friends: one must try to live in goodness and truth; "for the battle prize is glorious and there is great hope."[16] After what seems to have been a silent pause he then starts again in a different tone: "Certainly it would not be suitable for a reasonably thinking man to vouch with certainty that everything is exactly as I have described it."[17] But does this mean that Socrates consciously shatters the certainty that has arisen in his listeners or that Plato does not take the myth seriously? But what else could it mean? The answer: Socrates has not finished yet; the sentence continues as follows: ". . . but that *this or something like it* is the way it will be with our souls and their dwelling place: it seems to me worth daring to believe it – such daring is beautiful."[18] Through this continuation of the sentence the previous statement that it is "not exactly" the way things are acquires a completely clear meaning, namely, that we are dealing with the truth of *symbolic* speech, but quite definitely with the truth. Even the most orthodox interpretation of the biblical parables (of the wedding feast, the vine, the fig tree – and so on) must say the same: it is not exactly like that; and yet it is so very true that one can dare to live and die by it.

It is rationalistic narrowness simply to relegate

symbolic speech to the realm of fantasy and, for example, thinking of the *Timaeus*, to say that representing the creation of the world as a work of mastery shows "that Plato . . . is giving free rein to his poetic fantasy."[19] Certainly it is possible that the Socratic reservation ("not exactly as . . .") has still another profound meaning,[20] namely, that the mythical story – because it is *human* speech about divine things, spoken by men and comprehensible to men – necessarily appears like a "lie" *in comparison with God's own speech.* "Only the daimonic and the divine" – according to what it says in the *Republic*[21] – is completely free of lies [*a-pseudés*]." Such an interpretation would certainly fit in with Platonic thinking. But in no way does it suggest that myth should not be accepted by man as valid beyond all doubt – as truth which, while not absolute, is the ultimate attainable truth.

But we will have to go further and say that this admirable truth is never "dogma" for Plato. On the contrary, it always remains open for discussion, for further testing in dialectical conversation.[22] – This, I think, can mean two things, one of which I agree with and the other not.

If by the necessity of "further testing in dialectical conversation" is meant that the attempted interpretation – because symbolic speech, by its very nature, cannot give fully adequate expression to the meaning – never achieves, once and for all, a satisfactory result and therefore always has to begin again and remains in need of constant testing, this is not in the least an objection against its claim to be true. It is the most natural thing in the world that, for example, Christian theology, "in dialectical conversation" with modern science and in confrontation with the conclusions of research on evolution or with the astrophysical conception of the cosmos, sees itself challenged to find a more exact and deeper interpretation of the biblical account of creation or of the biblical statements about "heaven." But this continuously new testing in no way implies doubting the truth of God's word. On the contrary the aim is to achieve a purer understanding of this truth and to "save" it. – If, however, "testing in dialectical conversation" means formal critical discussion of actual truth (in myths), it must be said that, once he accepted (certainly not uncritically) a mythical story as sacred tradition, Plato never put it up for discussion in that sense.

What, then, can be said about Plato's unquestionable "critique of myth"? The most radical meaning that this term could have is that the mythical as such is not an adequate medium for expressing thought. Here is Hegel[23] again; and there is hardly any need expressly to show why this is exactly what Plato's "critique of myth" cannot mean. A further possibility would be to see it as an attempt to distinguish between levels of certainty in the mythical statement. This kind of distinction is definitely to be found in Plato. In *Phaedo*, for example, Socrates expresses his confidence that after death he will have the company of good and wise gods and also of good men; and then he adds: he is, of course, not quite so certain about the men as he is that he will meet with ruling *gods* who are full of goodness; "that is as certain as anything else of this kind."[24] Clearly, what is happening here is no undiscriminating, uncritically naïve acceptance of what is handed down. Where is there any trace of fundamental doubt about the truth of myth as such? A different thing again is the attempt, within the actual corpus of material handed down "from ages ago," to distinguish between – not the higher or lesser grades of their binding quality, but the true and the false, i.e., what is really mythical and what is not. Indeed, Plato devoted passionate energy to this "critical task." However, because under the conditions of pre-Christian thinking he was fundamentally in no position to succeed in the task, there is a sense of tragedy in his efforts, especially in his battle against the sophists. "Do you really think that something of this kind happened: . . . that the gods were at war with one another, that they were enemies of one another, that there were battles – and other things like this the way the poets relate them and the way we see them depicted in the images with which painters adorn our shrines? Are we to say, this is truth?" This is what Socrates says[25] to a priest who follows the letter of the law but has no concept of real devoutness. At that time Socrates had already been charged with godlessness; and he himself says that the reason lies perhaps more in the fact that he is filled with great indignation that "the gods are spoken about in this way."[26] Plato is here giving us to understand that it was for this very particular kind of "critique of myth" that Socrates went to his death – therefore, not because he denied a truth but because, against the unseriousness of unbridled fantasy, he defended the truth about the gods as it is revealed in legitimate sacred tradition.

But this also defines Plato's most genuine aim. This becomes completely clear in the second book of the *Republic*, which, on the other hand – as we know – is considered the classical counter-argument, namely, as a proof that Plato precisely did *not* see in myth in general a form of truth. This part of the *Republic*[27] deals with education of the guardians, and Socrates begins with a fundamental question: "Are we, without thinking, to let children hear myths which just anybody happens to think up?" His young partner in the conversation, Adeimantus, a brother of Plato, is not clear where this obviously polemical question is going, and Socrates elucidates: "I'm referring to the untruthful myths which Hesiod and Homer and the other poets think up and recount." (It is worth reflecting for a moment that, in *this* context, Plato uses the expression "lie-myth" [*mythos pseudés*) which has become so famous.) Adeimantus, somewhat taken aback by such aggressiveness, again asks which myths he has in mind and what is wrong with them. "In my opinion they speak badly about the way the gods really are – as when a painter paints a picture that does not resemble the person it is meant to represent."[28] And now follows a whole negative collection of quotations from Homer which distort the true nature of the gods instead of revealing it. Adeimantus asks where the true myths are to be found. He receives the answer: "We are, you and I, at this moment not poets but founders of a state [polis]. It is proper for such founders to know the archetypal images on which poets must base the stories they tell:"[29] "what God truly is – precisely that is what must be said of him."[30] "But God is, in truth, *good* – and consequently that is the way he must be spoken of."[31] – It is clear that Hegel's summarizing thesis[32] is completely correct: "He banishes poets from his state, because he finds their ideas of God unworthy."

This is the point to recall the important fact that criticism of Homeric theodicy was integral to philosophy many centuries before Plato. It is Xenophanes who says: "All that is disgraceful and blameworthy among men, stealing, adultery, and fraud: all that has been pinned on the gods by Homer and Hesiod."[33] These are Heraclitus' much more severe words: "Homer deserved to be chased away from the games and whipped."[34] Plato, too, is in line with them. It is hard for him, he says,[35] to say anything against Homer, whom he has loved and honored since childhood; "but truth is to be honored more than man, and I have to speak accordingly."

Here, as I well know, I have put an obstacle in the path of my own argument. Is there really, one could object, a distinction between true and false *within* the mythical tradition? Or does not Plato, on the contrary, oppose to the anthropomorphic stories about the gods a new *concept* of god which has been purified in the fire of philosophical reflection? To this I would answer that naturally and necessarily *both* are involved: on the one hand, the skepticism of the critically alert consciousness vis-à-vis the rank growth of naïve images of God; and, on the other hand, the claim of measuring the actual tradition in the light of "true" myth. It can easily be shown that this second element is also involved. When faced, for example, with the hopelessness of Homeric expectations for the afterlife which we sense in the despairing cry of Achilles, Plato does not counter with a philosophical argument but expressly with the inviolable truth of the eschatological myth. Precisely that is the meaning of the at-first-mysterious word with which the mythical story of the *Republic* begins: what now follows is "not an Alcinous story," by which is meant the Homeric story of Odysseus,[36] in which also the dead are conjured up and Achilles appears.

Incidentally, the usual idea of an extremely precise separation of concept from mythical truth is in need of correction. Certainly Plato saw the inclusion of the sacred tradition of myth as an element of philosophizing, perhaps even as the most crucial act of the philosopher. Both in *Gorgias* and in the *Republic* the eschatological myth is used as the last decisive argument after purely rational utterance has reached its own limit.

For Plato there is no question about myth's claim to truth. The extent of his conviction is expressed with particular energy in the comment with which Socrates, at the end of the *Republic*, concludes the story about reward and punishment in the next life: may the myth that is "saved" by the soldier who, on the funeral pyre, returns to life "also save us when we believe in it."[37] – It is a constant cause of astonishment to see how much learned subtlety has been spent on "proving" that Plato could not have said such things in all seriousness.[38] Certainly it is true that he uses words in this context which, spoken seriously, are extremely dangerous and explosive.

Sozein, according to the dictionaries, means: to cure, to make healthy, to keep alive, to preserve, to rescue, to bring to a happy conclusion; it is the word that in the Greek of the New Testament will mean "to save" [salvation]. It may be slightly confusing to encounter almost without warning, in the Platonic dialogue about the state, the thought that there could be such a thing as a message which contains a healing force. Of course, this force – and this, too, is said – does not work automatically through any kind of magic; instead, it works only for the believer. – And this is the second dangerous word: *peíthesthai*. Consulting the dictionaries again, you find it means more or less: to let oneself be convinced, moved, decided; to obey, to follow, to trust, to believe; this last meaning applies especially when the verb is used with a dative object – which is precisely the case here. The word *peíthesthai* occurs frequently in the Platonic dialogues and with the most varied meanings. It seems to thrive particularly well in the soil of the mythical stories. In relation to the *Phaedo* myth Socrates says no less than three times: *pépeismai*, "I have believed it."[39] The same form of the word occurs in the *Symposium* at a point where it has a particularly representative character: Socrates relates how Diotima, the priestly woman from Mantinea, initiated him into the mysteries of Eros; no proper conversation took place; Socrates himself did speak, but only as one who asks questions and learns. The lengthy description of all this ends with what understandably has been called a somewhat "un-Socratic" sentence: "This is the kind of thing Diotima said, but I believed it" [*pépeismai d'egó*].[40]

It is again very revealing to go through the German Plato editions looking for the translation of this word *peíthesthai*.[41] Each time it corresponds to what we have seen above. It is not surprising to find, with an author like Couturat,[42] that the word *peíthesthai* is regularly interpreted as meaning that Socrates is only expressing an opinion, anything but his conviction. But Wilamowitz is also not far from such an interpretation when he says[43] that Plato only introduced the Diotima figure so that "Socrates did not need to say anything that would be contradictory to his own inner self." In contrast to this, a more recent work on the Platonic myths about the afterlife arrives at the conclusion that *peíthesthai*, used in such a context, "means the certainty of faith."[44] This seems to me the only possible interpretation.

VI

IF IT IS THE CASE THAT PLATO BELIEVES IN THE TRUTH
of the myths he narrates, *who* is it that he believes? The really decisive element in the act of
faith[1] is not *what* is believed but the *someone* on
the basis of whose witness one accepts as valid
something one cannot, for oneself, verify as true.
The question about this someone is almost identical with the other question – already formulated
at the beginning of the book[2] – about the author
of the mythical narration and about the authority
on which it is based.

It has been said that "the soul" is the origin of
myths; "mythical births" have been attributed to
it:[3] "The soul conjures up a realm which has eternal laws and a system of judgment."[4] This seems
to me an all too vague statement. Far from answer-
ing the question, it hardly approaches an answer.
– Plato himself answers with more precision. The
authority that authenticates the myth – he says it
on innumerable occasions[5] – is the "ancients." Admittedly, he never gives an individual name; the

"ancients" remain anonymous. Yet he is referring to something quite exact. Men advanced in years, men of experience, the "old" men are not what he means. Nor does he mean the pioneers, the ones who break new ground, nor the "noble minds" praised by Hegel,[6] who, through the courageous use of their reason, have penetrated into the secret of the world. Rather, the "ancients" are those who were the first to receive and pass on the message which derives from a divine source.[7] When the Seventh Letter[8] calls "old and *holy*" the speech about immortality and judgment after death, it is clearly to be taken more literally than is always the case.

The "ancients" are likewise not the originators of the myth. They hand down nothing of their own, but a message they have received. The message itself is a "gift from the gods to mankind" [*theón eis anthrópous dosis*].[9] That is a clear and important statement at the extreme edge of what it was possible for Plato to say; and his own obscure word referring to a "certain" – therefore unidentifiable – Prometheus who brought down the message[10] seems to say that he is aware of this limit.

If one wishes to pursue the question about the originator of the myth beyond this point, one must realize that an answer cannot be had by way of an interpretation of Plato. This does not mean that an answer is not possible. What is required above all is readiness to pose the question more radically than has heretofore been the case. To say it more clearly: *really* to pose the question. This has not already happened through the attempt to find out what Plato, for his part, thinks about the truth of the myths he has narrated. Rather, the question is what we ourselves think of it, i.e., whether we ourselves are convinced there is reality in the things the myths speak of: the idea that all being proceeds from the ungrudging goodness of the Creator; the occurrence of primeval guilt and punishment; judgment on the other side of death. Naturally, it all depends on who is meant by "we." Insofar as the "we" means Christians, it is clear that the answer to the question of truth can only be: yes, there is reality in all of this!

The pure fact of this consensus is one of the most astounding things one can encounter in the history of ideas, and yet it seems possible to go a little beyond the purely factual and see something of the *basis* for the consensus.

Rooted in Christian theology from the earliest times is the concept which both clarifies and surpasses the Platonic idea of a message coming down to us from a divine source: the concept of "original revelation." If one attempts to summarize its content in the very briefest form, the following is the result: at the beginning of man's history a divine communication is made specifically for mankind; this communication became part of the sacred tradition of all peoples, part of their myths, and is preserved in them – admittedly distorted, overgrown with weeds, and often enough almost unrecognizable, yet, at the same time, never to be lost. This indestructible truth of mythical tradition stems, accordingly, from the same Logos [word] that in Christ became man. Only the light of this Logos that entered into man's history makes possible something that goes beyond the strength of pre-Christian thinking, namely, the clear distinction between true and false within the actual corpus of tradition, as well as the separation of the "true myth" from the shell of the accidental and irrelevant.

In two crucial points, however, we are not one step ahead of Socrates and Plato or anyone else.

First, only *ex akoés* can we, too, share the truth of that message which stems from a divine source – not through experience, or thinking, or verification, but only through believing.

Second, above all it is not given to the most

advanced mind to express this truth in terms of a conceptual thesis; on the contrary, it is irrevocably in the form of a story which is told to us. The reason for this is that we are expressly not – to use Lessing's words – dealing with "absolute truths of reason," which could be deduced from abstract principles, but with events and actions which derive from the freedom of God and of men.

In this regard there is no distinction between the statements that Christians believe and the myths recounted by Plato. Both have in common that their subject is not intellectual content but a story played out between the realm of the gods and the realm of men.

ENDNOTES

I

1   *Republic* 3606b5.
2   *Platons Lehre von der Wahrheit*, Bern 1947, p. 5.
3   *Republic* 614 ff.
4   "Über das *Symposium* des Platon." *Sitzungsberichte der Preußischen Akademie der Wissenschaften*, 21(1912), p. 333.
5   *Sämtliche Werke. Jubiläumsausgabe*, edited by Glockner, Stuttgart 1927–1940, vol. 18, p. 179.
6   *Phänomenologie des Geistes*, edited by Johannes Hoffmeister, Hamburg, 1952, p. 12.
7   *Luke* 10, 30.
8   Aristotle, *Poetics* 145a31.
9   I have used mainly Liddell-Scott's *Greek-English Lexicon*, Oxford 1958.
10 *Gorgias* 523a1.
11 *Republic* 376 f.
12 *Sophist* 242c.
13 *Republic* 565d.
14 *Ibid.*, 328–331.
15 *Ibid.*, 621b8.
16 Article "Mythos" in *Religion in Geschichte und Gegenwart*, 3rd edition, vol. 4, pp. 363 ff. – Similarly Karl Kerényi, *Die antike Religion*, Amsterdam 1940, pp. 38 f. – Walter Willi, who was one of the first to attempt a systematic presentation of the Platonic myths, says that the godhead is the only subject dealt with by myth; see his "Versuch einer Grundlegung der platonischen Mythopoiie," Zürich-Leipzig-Berlin 1925, p. 13. –

Karl Reinhardt says the same thing: "Almost everything that is mythical in Plato" is "somehow [to do with] the next world." *Platons Mythen*, Bonn 1927, p. 49.

17   *Gorgias* 524a.

18   Wilhelm Nestle says in a kind of definition: "To my mind, a clear concept of myth includes the three characteristics: narration, the supernatural sphere, and symbolic meaning." Quoted by Walter Willi in *Philosophische Wochenschrift*, 47 (1927), column 674.

19   *Vorlesungen über die Geschichte der Philosophie*, vol. 1, edited by Johannes Hoffmeister, Leipzig 1944, p. 211. On page 213: "When the mind can express itself in the sphere of thought, the symbolic is a wrong, false mode of expression."

20   *Die Philosophie der Griechen* II, 1; 4th edition, Leipzig 1889, pp. 580 f.

21   *Gorgias* 527a–b f.

22   *Statesman* 277d. – Dante says in his famous letter to Can Grande della Scala, in which he refers to the ambiguity of the *Divine Comedy*: "We see much with our minds without having the corresponding words. Plato makes this plain enough for us in his books by the way he resorts to speaking in parables. He sees much in the light of his intellect that he has not been able to express in appropriate speech, *sermone proprio*." And Goethe: "Philosophy, in its highest reaches, sometimes has to use inadequate expressions and parables." *Materialien zur Geschichte der Farben-lehre*, edited by Gunter Ipsen, Leipzig, Insel Verlag, p. 579.

23   Hans Leisegang, *Die Platondeutung der Gegenwart*, Karlsruhe 1929, p. 137.

24   *Wörterbuch der philosophischen Begriffe*, edited by Johannes Hoffmeister, 2nd edition, Hamburg, 1955, Article on "Mythos," p. 419. I include here some expressions found in scholarly Plato literature, all suggesting that the myths narrated by Plato were also created by him: "consciously speaking in parables."

(Paul Stöcklein, *Über die philosophische Bedeutung von Platons Mythen*, Leipzig, 1937, p. 6); "Der Mythenbildner Platon" (Hans Werner Thomas, *Epikeina. Untersuchungen über das Überlieferungsgut in den Jenseitsmythen Platons*, Würzburg 1938, p. 2.); "die eigenschöpferische Gestaltungskraft Platons in seiner Mythendichtung" (*ibid.*, p. 157); "l'oeuvre réfléchie d'un penseur" (Perceval Frutiger, *Les myths de Platon*, Paris 1930, p. 34); "a story shaped at will" (L. Edelstein, "The Function of the Myths in Plato's Philosophy," *Journal of History of Ideas*, vol. 10, 1949, p. 1466); "Der Mythos . . . von Platon erfunden" (Gerhard Müller, *Die Mythen der platonischen Dialoge. Nachrichten der Gießener Hochschulgesell-schaft*, 32[1963], p. 79).

25 Article "Mythe," vol. VI, column 2848.

II

1 *Phaedrus* 229e4.
2 Paul Friedländer, *Platon*, 2nd edition, vol. 3, Berlin 1960, p. 52.
3 *Theaetetus* 155d.
4 *Symposium* 203b.
5 *Maximen und Reflexionen*, edited von G. Müller, Kröners Taschenausgabe, numbers 633–634.
6 Frutiger, *Les mythes de Platon*, p. 180.
7 Willi, *Versuch einer Grundlegung der platonischen Mythopoiie*, p. 43 ("its – the art myth's – source is the poet Plato").
8 *Gorgias* 511d.
9 *Ibid.*, 493c.
10 *Ion* 533f.
11 *Theaetetus* 191 f.
12 *Republic* 515b.
13 See Willi, *Versuch einer Grundlegung*, p. 18.
14 *Crito* 54b.

15 *Phaedo* 62b.
16 Both Schleiermacher and Apelt give this translation of
    the passage (*Phaedo* 61d9).
17 *Statesman* 269b.
18 Friedländer, *Platon*, 2nd edition, vol. 1, p. 184.
19 A. Döring, *Die eschatologischen Mythen Platons. Archiv für die Geschichte der Philosophie*, 6(1893), p. 475.
20 R. Wiggers, *Beiträge zur Entwicklungsgeschichte des philosophischen Mythos bei den Griechen*, Rostock 1927, p. 20.
21 K. Reinhardt, *Platons Mythen*, p. 97.

III

1   Parmenides, Fragment 1, 29 (Diels).
2   See Friedländer, *Platon*, 2nd etdition, vol. 2, p. 253.
3   Reinhardt, *Platons Mythen*, p. 52.
4   See Willi, *Versuch einer Grundlegung*, pp. 47 f.
5   *Gorgias* 522c.
6   *Ibid.* 522e.
7   *Ibid.* 523a1.
8   *Ibid.* 524a8 f.
9   *Phaedo* 113d7.
10 *Gorgias* 525c6.
11 See Eckart Peterich, *Die Theologie der Hellenen*, Leipzig 1938, pp. 318 f.
12 *Ibid.* p. 378.
13 *Odyssey* 11, pp. 477 ff.
14 *Republic*, pp. 377–387.
15 L Couturat, *De mythis Platonicis*, p. 111.
16 *Phaedo* 107d.
17 *Ibid.*, 114a–b.
18 *Ibid.*, 114c1.
19 *Ibid.*, 111b7 f.
20 Otto Apelt in the notes to his *Phaedo* translation, Leipzig 1923, p. 150.
21 *Ibid.*

IV

1 R. Wiggers, *Beiträge zur Entwicklungsgeschichte des philosophischen Mythos bei den Griechen*, p. 25.

2 L. Couturat, *De platonicis mythis*, Paris 1896, p. 19.

3 W. Windelband, *Platon*, 7th edition, Stuttgart 1923, p. 122.

4 Gerhard Krüger, *Einsicht und Leidenschaft. Das Wesen des platonischen Denkens*, 2nd edition, Frankfurt 1948, p. 130.

5 *Ibid.*, pp. 123 ff.

6 *Symposium* 189d6.

7 See *Symposium* 189c–193d.

8 *Timaeus* 33b.

9 *Symposium* 190e1

10 Frutiger, *Les mythes de Platon Gorgias*, pp. 237 ff.

11 *Maximen und Reflexionen*, edited by G. Müller, no. 1372.

12 See G. von Loeper in "Goethes Sprüche in Prosa," Munich, n.d., p. 149.

13 *Symposium* 193a.

14 *Sophist* 265c2.

15 *Ibid.*, 266c5.

16 *Ibid.*, 266b4.

17 *Timaeus* 28c3–4.

18 *Ibid.*, 29c1.

19 *Ibid.*, 37c7.

20 *Ibid.*, 29b1–2.

21 *Ibid.*, 28a6–7.

22 *Ibid.*, 29a2–3.

23 *Ibid.*, 29d5–30a5.

24 *Ibid.*, 31b3; similarly 55d4. – Just how closely the notion of the one world is in fact linked with the idea of creation becomes very clear, in a negative way, in Nicolai Hartmann's thesis, according to which it is "meaningless" and an "illusion" to speak of the unified nature of the world once belief in a creator has disappeared. See Hartmann, *Neue Wege der Ontologie in "Systema-*

tische Philosophie," edited by N. Hartmann, Stuttgart
and Berlin 1932, p. 245 (47).

25 *Phaedo* 111b7.

26 *Revelation* 21, 3.

V

1   Published 1927.

2   Here he is alluding to the title of a work by Wilamowitz,
"Der Glaube der Hellenen," 1931, newly published by
the Wissenschaftlich Buchgesellschaft, Darmstadt
1955.

3   At the beginning of the preface to his *Theodicy*.

4   Vol. 1: *Die Philosophie des Altertums*, 12th edition,
Berlin 1926, p. 315.

5   Karl Prümm, *Religionsgeschichtliches Handbuch für
den Raum der altchristlichen Umwelt*, Freiburg 1943,
p. 99.

6   Seventh Letter 335a3–4.

7   *Timaeus* 40d.

8   See R.J. Woltjer, *De Platone Praesocraticorum philo-
sophorum existimatore et judice*. Lugduni Batavorum,
1904, pp. 178–184.

9   O. Willmann, *Geschichte des Idealismus*, 2nd edition,
Braunschweig 1907, vol.1, pp. 416 ff.

10 *Ibid.*, p. 419. Perhaps Willmann was not correct to
refer to Constantin Ritter and Leopold Schmidt as cor-
roboration for this opinion.

11 Chantepie de la Saussaye, *Lehrbuch der Religionsge-
schichte*, 2nd edition, Freiburg 1897, vol. 2, p. 349.

12 *Die Philosophie der Griechen* II,1; p. 932.

13 P. Friedländer, *Platon*, 1st edition, vol. 1, p. 219.

14 *Ibid.* – It needs to be said that, in the second edition of
the work which appeared twenty-five years later,
Friedländer modified this formulation somewhat.
In vol. 1, p. 201, he writes that "here truth is mixed
with poetic invention." However, although the term

pseudos is no longer used, the thesis remains fundamentally unaltered. "This return to uncertainty is really of the essence of myth" (*ibid.*).

15 Two examples chosen at random can suffice: In the section of *Phaedo* under discussion here, Socrates says that in the hour of death one must be pondering, cast a spell on oneself, cure oneself of one's fear: "That is the very reason that I linger over this myth." (114d7). In the Apelt version (*der Philosophischen* Bibliothek) this sentence is rendered as follows: "That is why I linger so long over this poetic description" (p. 128). – The second example stems from the *Timaeus* translation of Franz Susemihl, recently included in the three-volume Plato edition published by Lambert Schneider, Heidelberg (vol. 3, p. 108). Here it is said that human reason cannot attain to definite knowledge of the gods and of the cosmos, so that, where there is credible myth [*eikóta mython*] about these things, nothing further may be sought [*Timaeus* 29d2]. This is translated as follows: "As long as the literary work has probability on its side."

16 *Phaedo* 114c8.

17 *Ibid.*, 114d1.

18 *Ibid.*, 114d6.

19 K. Praechter, *Philosophie des Altertums*, Überweg, vol. 1, p. 315.

20 Friedländer, too, points to this: *Platon*, 2nd edition, vol. 1, p. 220.

21 *Republic* 382e6.

22 Friedländer, *Platon*, 2nd edition, vol. 2, p. 253.

23 Hegel, *Vorlesungen über die Geschichte der Philosophie*, edited by Johannes Hoffmeister, vol. 1, p. 213.

24 *Phaedo* 63c4.

25 *Euthyphro* 6b–c.

26 *Ibid.*, 66b.

27 *Republic* 377b5 ff.

28 *Ibid.*, 377e1–3.

29 *Ibid.*, 378e7 f.

30 *Ibid.*, 379a7.

31 *Ibid.*, 379b1.

32 *Vorlesungen über die Geschichte der Philosophie, Sämtliche Werke*, vol. 18, p. 287.

33 H. Diels, *Die Fragmente der Vorsokratiker*, 7th edition, edited by W. Kranz, Berlin 1954, vol. 1, p. 132.

34 *Ibid.*, vol. 1, p. 160.

35 *Republic* 595c2.

36 Plato had already mentioned it and made his judgment about it [*Republic* 386–387]. See also Apelt's commentary in his translation of the *Republic* (Philos. Bibliothek); 7th edition, Leipzig 1944, p. 539, note 53.

37 *Republic* 621c1.

38 For example, Willi writes (*Versuch einer Grundle-gung der platonischen Mythopoiie*, p. 48) that it is a joking use of the "familiar fairytale ending," which, of course, has slight individual variations; and also, incidentally, "the naïve style" has to be looked at – achieved by the frequent use of the word "and."

39 *Phaedo* 108e1; 108e4; 109e7.

40 *Symposium* 212b1.

41 In the usual translations three different formulations are to be found: "That is what Diotima said; I have been won over" (Kurt Hildebrandt in the *Symposium* edition of the *Philosophische Bibliothek*, 4th edition, Leipzig 1922, p. 92); "Diotima spoke such things and she convinced me" (Wilhelm Nestle in Kröner's pocket edition of Plato's "Hauptwerke," Stuttgart 1931, p. 133); similarly Franz Susemihl in the *Gesamtausgabe* published by Lambert Schneider, vol. 1, p. 711. Schleiermacher, as well as Franz Boll and Bruno Schnell say: "I believed her."

42 *De Platonicis Mythis*, p. 23.

43 Wilamowitz, *Platon. Sein Leben und seine Werke*, edited by Bruno Schnell, Berlin-Frankfurt 1948, p. 298.

44 H.W. Thomas, *Epekeina*, p. 84, note 135.

VI

1 See Josef Pieper, *Über den Glauben*, Munich, 1962, pp. 26 ff.
2 See pp. 25 f.
3 K. Reinhardt, *Platons Mythen*, p. 43.
4 *Ibid.*, p. 49.
5 See Josef Pieper, *Über den Begriff der Tradition*, Cologne-Opladen 1958 (*Tradition: Concept and Claim*, South Bend, Ind., 2010), pp. 20 ff.
6 *Vorlesungen über die Geschichte der Philosophie*, edited by Johannes Hoffmeister, p. 6.
7 *Philebus* 16c5–6.
8 Seventh Letter 335a.
9 *Philebus* 16c5.
10 *Ibid.*, 16c6.

INDEX

Index

Hebrews, xiii
Hegel, G.W.F., 3–4, 10, 50, 52, 59; *Vorlesungen über die Geschichte der Philosophie*, 69
Heidegger, Martin, 2
Heraclitus, 53
Hesiod, xi, 52–53
Hildebrandt, Kurt, 71
Hobbes, Thomas, xv
Homer, xi, 24–25, 52–54

Iris, 13
Isle of the Blessed, 26–29, 42, 47

judgment after death, 6–7, 10, 21, 30, 42, . *See also* myth: eschatological myths; Plato's dialogues: *Gorgias*, myth of judgment after death.
justice and injustice, 22–24

Kerényi, Karl; *Die antike Religion*, 63
Krüger, Gerhard, *Einsicht und Leidenschaft. Das Wesen des platonischen Denkens*, 67

Leibniz, Gottfried, 42,
Leisegang, Hans; *Die Platondeutung der Gegenwart*, 64

Lessing, Gotthold Ephraim, 62
literature, 3
Logos, 61

Machiavelli, Niccolò, xv
Müller, Gerhard, *Die Mythen der platonischen Dialoge. Nach richten der Gießener Hochschulgesellschaft*, 65
myth, xvi, 4–14, 15, 18–21, 28–29, 41–42, 44, 46, 49, 58, 60; two sorts of: teach a lesson by example, xii; explain the origins of man and his relation to God, xii, 7–8, 16, 31–36, 42; eschatological, xv–xvii, 8, 16, 19, 21–23, 26–27, 54–55, 57; as essential in Plato's philosophy, xi; as narrative, not creation, 11–13; as allegory, 14; as artistic, 14; and tradition, 18; cosmological, 29, 39; and hearing. *See* hearing.

Nestle, Wilhelm, 64, 71
New Testament, 4, 40, 47; Good Samaritan, parable of the, 4
Nicene Creed, xviii

Index